Margaret Stokes, Royal Irish Academy

The High Crosses of Castledermot and Durrow

Margaret Stokes, Royal Irish Academy

The High Crosses of Castledermot and Durrow

ISBN/EAN: 9783337299705

Printed in Europe, USA, Canada, Australia, Japan

Cover: Foto ©Andreas Hilbeck / pixelio.de

More available books at **www.hansebooks.com**

THE HIGH CROSSES

CASTLEDERMOT AND DURROW

WITH TWELVE ILLUSTRATIONS

BY

MARGARET STOKES

HONORARY MEMBER OF THE ROYAL IRISH ACADEMY

PUBLISHED AT THE ACADEMY HOUSE, 19, DAWSON STREET

By HODGES, FIGGIS, & CO. (Ltd.), GRAFTON STREET

By WILLIAMS & NORGATE

LONDON: 14, HENRIETTA STREET, COVENT GARDEN

EDINBURGH: 20, SOUTH FREDERICK STREET.   OXFORD: 7, BROAD STREET

THE Photogravure Plate consists of the reproduction of the quarter-plate Photographs of the East and West faces of the Castledermot Crosses, from which were taken the enlargements which formed the basis of Miss Stokes's Illustrations. (See Introduction, p. ii.) One of Miss Stokes's quarter-plates of the Durrow Cross having been lost, the Publication Committee of the Royal Irish Academy directed Photographs of the Cross to be taken; the East and West faces are represented on the Plate, the North and South sides will be found on page 12.

DUBLIN: PRINTED AT THE UNIVERSITY PRESS, BY PONSONBY AND WELDRICK.

THE HIGH CROSSES OF IRELAND.

INTRODUCTION.

AMONG the various monuments of early Christian Art still left in Ireland, none are possessed of greater interest than the sculptured High Crosses standing within the precincts of many ancient monasteries throughout the country. The form of these crosses is peculiar, and may be held to have originated in Ireland, where the Eastern form of the Cross within a circle was changed to a Latin Cross *with* the circle, by lengthening the central line so as to form a shaft or pillar, and by extending the arms and head beyond the circle.* This form appears to have remained fixed in Ireland, contemporaneously with that of the Round Towers, from the ninth, if not eighth, to the twelfth century. It is true that occasional instances of this type occur in the north of England and south of Scotland; but the words of Mr. Anderson,† in reference to the occasional Round Towers of Scotland, may, I think, with equal justice be applied to the occasional High Crosses in Great Britain. He says of these Round Towers, that they are "stragglers from a great typical group which has its *habitat* in Ireland"; and therefore he adds: "It follows from this, that all questions as to the origin, purpose, and period of the type must be discussed with reference to the evidence derived from the investigation of the principal group, and that the general conclusions drawn from the extended data furnished by the *many in Ireland* must hold good for the *few* in Scotland."

It is therefore in the interests of comparative Archæology that some effort should be made for the publication of a complete series of faithful illustrations of these ancient Irish monuments, which are inscribed with the mystic language of early Christian Art.

These monuments appear to have belonged exclusively to Sanctuaries; and in twenty-nine instances they are associated with Round Towers or their acknowledged sites.

I know already of thirty-seven High Crosses with circles still preserved. To these may be added nine shafts of Crosses that appear to have had circles. There are four High Crosses without circles, i.e. Latin Crosses with Irish decorative patterns. Five others are not described.

The distribution of these High Crosses, in the Irish counties, is as follows:

Antrim,	1.	Down,	4.	King's,	4.	Meath,	8.
Armagh,	7.	Galway,	3.	Louth,	4.	Sligo,	2.
Carlow,	2.	Kildare,	4.	Londonderry,	2.	Wicklow,	2.
Clare,	2.	Kilkenny,	7.	Monaghan,	1.	Waterford,	2.

---

* A cross described to me by Mr. Pitt Kennedy (April, 1898) bears a marked resemblance to the Irish type (it may be seen at Plougoumelen, seven kilomètres from Auray, Morbihan), but instead of the upper limb of the Cross passing through the wheel, there are two small Crosses on the top of it.

† J. Anderson, *Scotland in early Christian Times.* Edinburgh: 1881, p. 49.

Beside these, I have the names of twenty-three monuments said to be High Crosses, which I have had no means of verifying. As yet I have heard of no Crosses of the circular type in Cavan, Cork, Leitrim, Limerick, or Longford.

These Monuments offer in their successive panels a series of subjects which can only be explained by the same method as that which foreign antiquaries have followed in the interpretation of the Sculptures on the façades and porches and stained glass windows of the great Cathedrals of France or Milan, or the Certosa of Pavia—or in the frescoes of Giotto and Simone Memmi, or the host of early Christian wall-painters in Europe, or in the Mosaics of the still greater host of Byzantine workers.

This method is based on the systems of image-writing—iconography,—that grew out of the necessity of teaching the salient truths of Christianity before printing was invented, and before the masses had learned to read. The grammar of this Art-language can only be learned by the study of such works as the Byzantine Painter's Guide; "The Speculum Humanæ Salvationis," ed. J. Ph. Berjeau; "The Biblia Pauperum," ed. J. Ph. Berjeau; and such illustrated copies of the Bestiaries of the early Christian period as can be procured.

In these works the events recorded in the Bible were treated not only as historic, but, when selected from the Old Testament, as prophetic of Christ, and as symbolic when taken from the New. The events recorded were turned to symbols. A system of such symbols was developed expressive of Christian truths. A hieratic cycle of subjects came into use, not necessarily for doctrinal purposes, but as expressive of religious faith.

In addition to the knowledge and understanding of this language, the Interpreter of the Art upon the Irish Crosses should come equipped, not only with knowledge of the method of teaching the Bible message by type and antitype; but also he should be acquainted with the history of the founder or first bishop of the Church to which the Cross belonged, events in whose life have occasionally been illustrated in one panel of the monument; and, lastly, he should have had experience in tracing the intricate designs and characteristic patterns of Irish Art. And yet he must often be prepared to confess himself quite baffled in the effort to decipher some of the subjects in these panels. In such cases the desire is strong to *compare*, or to enable foreign antiquaries to compare, these sculptures with similar subjects abroad, and the only way this can be done is by the circulation of faithful illustrations.

Here I may be allowed to explain the way I have followed in the illustration of these monuments with all their detail.

It seemed best to sacrifice all pictorial or landscape effect, and not to throw the monument into perspective, but to keep in sight the single object of distinct reproduction; therefore, I photographed the four sides of each cross as much in the front view as the nature of the ground allowed. I waited through the day till the sun had illuminated each side in succession if not prevented by overshadowing trees; I then made ½-plate photographs of each side, which I afterwards enlarged and printed on platino-type paper. Having mounted these, so that they would bear touching with a fine sable brush and Indian ink, I returned to the monument. Then, having the help of friends whose skill in deciphering patterns often exceeded my own—such antiquaries as Lord Walter Fitz Gerald, Mr. Geo. Coffey, and

Dr. Healy of Kells,—careful rubbings were made of every separate panel, those at the summit of the monument being taken with much pain and trouble from the tops of ladders, and finally the whole photograph was gone over with touches of white in the high lights and black in the shadows.

It is quite a mistake to suppose that the photograph alone will ever truly represent all the art upon these crumbling and timeworn monuments. The lichens that catch the light or make white stains on the surface, often confuse the intricate knots and windings of the sculpture—the cracks in the stone confuse the incised patterns; and the eye itself is not to be trusted where the reliefs on the stone are as worn and smoothed away as they are, for example, on the west face of Castledermot South Cross, where they are scarcely distinguishable to the eye till the sun casts a side-light on the monument. At such moments it becomes the duty of the antiquary to catch and fix these fleeting gleams and perpetuate all the detail that they reveal. This again has to be corrected by reference to rubbings and by feeling the pattern over with the finger so as to avoid being misled by lichens and the blemishes already referred to. The priceless benefit of the photograph in such instances is, that it not only gives the texture of the stone, but also a firm and trustworthy foundation on which to work.

As regards the letterpress accompanying the following illustrations, I have adopted the following uniform plan :—

      1st. Situation.
      2nd. Name.
      3rd. Founder of Church near Cross. Existing remains of Monastery.
      4th. Description of Cross, material, size, etc.
      5th. Analysis and interpretation of figures in panels.
      6th. Ornamental designs in panels.
      7th. Ancient references to Cross.
      8th. Existing legends connected with Cross.
      9th. Present condition and position or place of Cross.
      10th. Previous illustrations of Cross, if any.

In the analysis given in the following pages of the sculptures on the North Cross of Castledermot, an example is given of the success of following a systematic method of interpretation, instead of venturing on haphazard guess-work.

Here the Scriptural message of Redemption commences, as prescribed in the Painter's Guide of Mount Athos,* with a figure of Death awakened in the tomb by the sound of the Gospel message. This figure is a prelude to the drama which opens at the Fall of Man on the central panel of the west face of the Cross. Redemption is prefigured by the sacrifice of Isaac; triumph over suffering by Daniel in the den of lions. Martyrdom by the crucifixion of St. Peter head-downwards. The Lord's Supper is typified by the miracle of the loaves and fishes, and by Melchisedek holding plate and chalice before

---

* See *Christian Iconography*: Didron, ed. Margaret Stokes: Appendix, vol. ii., p. 318 : " How to represent the Holy Passion."

Abraham. On the east side is the final Act of Redemption—the Death of Christ,—with the Church bearing witness to it in the forms of the twelve Apostles arranged in groups of three around it.

The treatment of this subject—the great drama of Redemption,—is not exactly the same on any two crosses that I have yet seen—yet *all* the subjects, except the illustrations of local legend, are among those prescribed in the books above mentioned.

But just as the Byzantine wall-painters occasionally introduce their local saints, so did the Irish sculptors illustrate scenes from the lives of the Irish saints which were typical of their ministration here, and the memory of which was thought worthy of record in stone. It happens often that one panel—at the top of the shaft close under the circle,—is devoted to some scene in the founder's or first abbot's life. Such may be traced on the shafts of the Crosses at Kilcullen in the County of Kildare, at Duleek in the County of Louth, and at Kinnetty in King's County.

The first bishop of Kilcullen was MacTáil, so called because he was the son of a wright; and in the Notes in the "Lebar Brecc" to the Martyrology of Oengus (ed. W. Stokes, p. ci), we read: "Because he took the wright's tál (adze), ... 'Son of Adze' he was called thenceforward." ("Tripartite Life of Patrick," p. 250.) Again, we learn that, among the wonders wrought by Patrick and his disciples, the bells made by MacTáil are enumerated (*op. cit.*, p. 185), and also that when Patrick went over into the plain of the Liffey, he placed this MacTáil over Kilcullen. In the upper panel of the shaft of the High Cross at Kilcullen, we see a figure of a bishop with his crozier and book, who holds an axe in his hand and whose bell hangs beside him. We may well believe that here the first bishop of the Church is represented.

A local subject is found on the Cross of Duleek, in the Church of Cianan. Adamnan is said to have visited the tomb of Cianan, where, owing to the prayer of Cairnech of Tulane, the body lay uncorrupted. "Comely is the body," said he, "and I beseech God then that it may be thus for ever, without dissolving till Christ shall come to the great assembly of doom! Only once a year, on Maunday, was the tomb to be opened and the hair and nails of the dead were cut; but Adamnan did not wait, and went in to touch the body. Thereupon his eye was struck out. So then he fasted to Cairnech and his eye was returned to him." ("Lebar Brecc," Mart. Oengus, p. clxxi.) This legend, and the restoration of the eye, are illustrated in the top panel of the eastern face of the Cross.

An episode in the life of Finan Camm seems to be illustrated on the topmost panel of the cross which stood in a church of his foundation at Kinnetty, in King's County. It is the story of the mission of Finan Camm. He had been a disciple and fellow-worker of Brendan of Clonfert, and after Brendan had seen the vision of angels in the cave of Fenit, "from that time forward no one save only Finan could look at Brendan's face, because of the abundance of the divine radiance, for Finan was himself full of the grace of the Holy Spirit." But the day came when Brendan saw that one or other of them must go forth from their common home in Clonfert and found a fresh monastery.

"Father," said Finan, "I am the younger: bless me, and send me forth on the journey." Then Brendan brought his pet bird to him and, blessing him, told Finan to follow the flight of the bird until it stopped, and that there where it rested he should found his new church. And so it happened that the bird guided him southwards to Kinnetty, in King's County, as we read in the Notes to the Martyrology of Oengus :—

" *Cell-Eti*, i.e. from the flying (eti) of the pet scald-crow which Brendan sent before him from the North from Cluain-ferta Brenainn."

On the highest panel of the shaft of the Cross taken from Kinnetty Church-yard and now set up in Castle Bernard demesne, we see the mission of Finan Camm represented : St. Brendan, seated, gives a crozier to the kneeling Finan, while the bird is seen hovering above their heads.

Notwithstanding the ravages of time, hints as to ancient costume may also be derived from a study of the figures on these Crosses. In the topmost panel of the side of the shaft of Durrow Cross, close under the shelter of the left arm, there is a tolerably preserved figure of an old Irish warrior seated wearing a diadem with bosses on the ears, like the head ornaments in the museum of the Royal Irish Academy. He has his spear and sword and circular shield, and a wolf-dog stands at each side of him.

However, illustrations such as these are of comparatively rare occurrence. The usual subjects found on the sculptured panels of these Crosses are those common to the early Christian art of mediæval Europe, the "Quatuor novissima"—the four last things : Death and Judgment—Heaven and Hell. One face of the Cross is generally devoted to the subject of the Death and Passion of Christ, in type and antitype ; the other to His Resurrection and Triumph in Heaven, when He is shown standing in the midst, and lifting up the blossoming rod of Aaron in His right hand, the Cross in His left. On the arms of the Cross, the joys of Heaven are represented. An unusual treatment of this subject is found on the Cross of Killamery. The Crucifixion, with the Dove brooding over the head of our Lord, is surmounted by a circular device, suggestive of the wheel—a symbol of Eternity ; and, on the arms, we find a hunting-scene on one side, and a chariot procession on the other. May not these sculptures be read as symbolising Eternity and the joys of Heaven ?

Such scenes as those represented on the arms of this Cross, if signifying the joys of Heaven to the Celtic mind of the tenth century, would harmonise with Virgil's description of Æneas on the Elysian fields, when he viewed with awe the heroes of old times :—

> " Their arms, their empty chariots, their war-spears,
> Set upright in the ground, their steeds unyoked,
> And grazing at their ease along the plains.
> The same delight in chariots and in arms,
> The same fond care in pasturing stock steeds,
> Which in their lives they had, they have in Death."
>
> ÆNEID, pp. 30, 31, Bk. VI., lines 885–890.
>
> *Translated by Sir Theodore Martin.*

We know that, in other instances, pagan forms and ideas lived on in the Christian Art of these islands long after they had died out elsewhere ; such festive scenes and long processions of chariots and horsemen are of common occurrence on the bases of these Irish Crosses ; and the example at Killamery, of the association of a procession and a hunting-scene with the Crucifixion of our Lord on the arms of the Cross, helps to confirm the belief that some religious meaning was attached to these figures. I can only repeat what I have said elsewhere, that it seems quite possible that these groups of huntsmen, animals, trumpeters, and harpers found on Irish Crosses, may belong to visions of a future state resembling that of Tennyson' seer:—

> "These eyes will find
> The men I knew, and watch the chariot whirl
> About the goal again, and hunters race
> The shadowy lion, and the warrior kings
> In height and prowess more than human, strive
> Again for glory, while the golden lyre
> Is ever sounding in heroic ears."

I have already spoken of these monuments as Sanctuary Crosses. The following details of the ancient Irish law of Sanctuary are given in the translation of the Brehon Law Tracts* :—

"The church protects sinners so that they come out of it free or bond, as they entered it, for although . . . it shelters the trespassers, or the sinners are sheltered in the church until they come out of it, . . ."

Then we have this note on the law of Sanctuary, i.e. violation to a person in regard of his protection (or, in Irish, his violation):—

"The running of the compensation is as far as three persons and the track of a host, i.e. the fine of the track of an army is here in the law of Sanctuary, and for arson, and it is not in Cáin law, or in Cairde law.

"*Precincts.* The running of 'Cairde law' and of the law of Sanctuary is to thrice nine persons, i.e. seven 'cumhals' for every hand as far as thrice nine persons. The running of Cairde law, i.e. a cumhal for every hand as far as thrice nine persons in the law of Sanctuary."

At page 60 of his work on "The Ecclesiastical Architecture of Ireland," Dr. Petrie speaks, without giving any reference, of "an ancient Canon of the Church," in obedience to which Crosses "were always erected to mark the limits of the Nemhedh, or Sanctuary." Mr. Warren has kindly suggested to me that he may have here meant the following Canon of the Hibernensis, Lib. xliv., Col. 3 † :—

"*De termino sancti loci ignoto,‡ terminatoque tribus personis.*

"*Sinodus Hibernensis :* Terminus sancti loci habeat signa circa se.

"*Sinodus dicit :* Ubicumque inveneritis signum crucis Christi, ne laeseritis. *Item :* Tres personae consecrant terminum loci sancti, rex, episcopus, populus."

---

* *Ancient Laws of Ireland,* vol. iv., p. 285.

† Wasserschleben, H.: *Die Irische Kanonensammlung.* Zweite Auflage : Leipzig, 1885 : p. 175.

‡ The meaning of this word "ignoto" being here obscure, I consulted Dr. Bernard and Mr. Warren on the question. They both agree in the opinion that it must stand, as there is no variation in the manuscripts at this point. It is a very curious word to use, but in all probability the phrase means something of this sort:—"About the otherwise unknown boundary of a holy place"; i.e., if it were not for the Crosses which are put to mark the boundary of the Sanctuary, the limits of the place of Sanctuary would be unknown. There is an interesting various reading for the first clause, "Terminus sancti loci habeat signa circa," out., (let the boundary of the Sanctuary have signs around it), in the Codex Valicellianus, a tenth-century MS. of the Hibernensis, viz., "Omnes sanctorum locorum termini consecrati debent habere signa circa, etc. et a plebilium agris separantur."

Translation: "Concerning the boundary of the Holy Place (the limits of the Sanctuary) unknown (?) and marked out by three persons.

"The Irish Synod: 'Let the boundary of the Sanctuary have signs around it.'

"The Synod saith: 'Wherever you may find the sign of the Cross of Christ, injure it not. Also: Three persons (representative) consecrate the boundary of the Sanctuary, viz., the King, the Bishop, the People.'"

It will be well now to consider such references to this custom of setting up a cross as a sign or mark as may be found in the "Annals of the Four Masters," and in those of "Ulster," "Clonmacnois," "Loch Cé," and in the "Chronicon Scotorum," as well as in such ancient tales as those contained in the "Dindsenchas," or in that of the "Boromean Tribute," or in the Lives of St. Patrick and other saints. In two instances out of the number of such entries, we find St. Patrick marking a rock near the site of a church with the sign of a cross. There is one set up as if a wayside cross by the pilgrim Fergus, and one sepulchral placed by St. Patrick over a Christian's grave. All the other entries refer to a class of monuments such as the columns and pillar-stones of antiquity, and they support the view that they were set up to mark the boundary of the Sanctuary or Termon, and refuge was ensured or at least promised to the fugitive beneath their shadow. The Crosses at Clonmacnois are distinguished by the names ("Ann. Four Masters," vol. ii., pp. 677, 879): "Cros Ard," or "The High Cross," and the "Cros na Screaptra," or "The Cross of the Scriptures." The Cross of Comgall at Clonmacnois (op. cit., vol. ii., p. 901) is also mentioned by the annalists and the author of the tale of the Convention of Taillte (see "Silva Gadelica," translated by Standish H. O'Grady, p. 453) as placed at the end of the causeway, and close by Comgall's ridge. A fourth Cross at Clonmacnois was styled the Cross of Bishop Etchen. (Op. cit., vol. ii., p. 901.) Five Crosses are also mentioned in the "Annals of the Four Masters" (op. cit., vol. ii., p. 1157), as belonging to Armagh Monastery, Columcille's, Bishop Eoghan's, Sechnall's, and the Cross of Brigid (op. cit., vol. ii., p. 1157), and another at the door of the Fort; and we read of the seizure of certain fugitives taken captive at the Cros na Screaptra at Clonmacnois in 1060, who appear to have taken refuge there.

In the "Lebar Brecc," Hua Suanaig's Cross is clearly spoken of as a monument of protection; it was also named "Cross of the Satirists." It belonged to the Church of Rahen, and a company of satirists who were attacked and pursued by a certain Mael-bresail, sought protection under this Cross. But Mael-bresail outraged that Cross: "Hence it is named the Cross of the Satirists."[*]

Ua Suanaigh's Cross, at Rathain, was erected as well to mark the boundaries of the Sanctuary as for a memorial of the re-erection of the Churches there.

In the account of the foundation of a monastery in the barony of Forth, county of Wexford, we read: Oct. 1, "When St. Fintan, or Munnu, was in the woods (in the barony of Forth, Wexford), he saw three men clothed in white garments, who told him 'Here will be your city,' and they marked out in his presence seven places in which afterwards the chief buildings of his city should be erected, AND FINTAN PLACED CROSSES THERE."[†]

---

* See Lebar Brecc (Notes on Martyrology of Oengus, p. lxxxvii).   † See Dict. of National Biography, vol. xix., p. 48.

There were also the five crosses at the monastery of Armagh, already specified by name, the site of one of which, and the site of the Cross at the door of the Rath, have been both identified. They stood to the north-east and south-east of the enclosure.

We read in the Life of St. Columba[*]: "He founded a church in the place where Swords standeth to-day. . . . Then he marked out the well named 'Sord,' that is, pure, and sained a Cross. For it was his wont to make Crosses, and writing-tablets, and book-satchels, and other church-gear. Now he sained three hundred Crosses, and three hundred wells, and a hundred tablets, and a hundred crosiers, and a hundred satchels."

In some instances we get particulars as to the position of such monuments in the Cashel. Thus in the "Annals of the Four Masters," A.D. 1156, mention is made of one of the high Crosses at Kells being placed in front of the door of the ante-temple, or *erdam*, and again one of the High Crosses of Clonmacnois stood at the end of the causeway leading from the ante-temple or erdam of St. Ciaran's Church: A.D. 1070, 4. M. Also, in the year 957, we read in the "Annals of the Four Masters": "The Termon (Sanctuary) of Ciaran was burned this year, from the High-Cross to the Shannon, both corn and mills."

In Armagh, one of the monuments was called "The Cross at the door of the fort"; and we find, in the account given by the Four Masters of the burning of Armagh in 1196, that the Rath, Trian, and Churches of Armagh came between the Cross of Brigid and the great Church, the Cross being outside the Rath.

In the "Rennes Dindsenchas,"[†] pt. 1, where Tara is described, we read (par. 18): "The site of *Adamnan's Pavilion* is in that fort (of the synods), and his Cross before that fort to the east, and his Seat and his Mound to the south of (his) Cross." And again (par. 20): "The site of the house which was burnt over Benén, (St.) Patrick's servant, and over Lucat Moel, (King) Loeguire's wizard, is a short distance to the south-east of Adamnán's Cross, beside the path a little to the east."

Again, in Tirechan's Collections in the "Book of Armagh," we read: "Et perrexit Patricius ad fontem qui dicitur Mucna.[‡] . . . Et est Signum Crucis in eo loco usque in hunc diem." The story is told also in the "Tripartite Life," p. 111: "And Patrick went to Mucno's well and erected Senchell. And Secundinus was there apart under a lofty elm; and the Sign of the Cross is in that place even to this day." The Saint erected a standing Cross at one place, as we learn from the following passage from Tirechan: "Extendit manum et indicavit ei locum in quo sunt ossa eius procul, et digito suo signavit locum et crucem posuit ibi."[§]

The following legend would seem to indicate that the base of a High Cross was a place where offerings might be laid. It is found in the Life of St. Findian of Clonard, in the Lives of Saints from the "Book of Lismore" (p. 224), where we read that "Bresal's hand after he was slain was brought by a hawk, which laid it down in Findian's presence at Cross Sailech"; this Bresal having profanely seized the cleric's hand to restrain him from building his church near a certain pig-sty and apple-tree in Leinster.

[*] W. Stokes: *Lives of the Saints, from the Book of Lismore*, pp. 177 sq.   [‡] *Tripartite Life*, p. 79.
[†] "Rennes Dindsenchas," *Revue Celtique*, vol. xv., No. 8, p. 286.   [§] *Op. cit.*, p. 820.

If St. Patrick cannot be said to have always erected such High Crosses in or around the Sanctuary when laying the foundations of a monastery, he certainly appears to have been in the habit of cutting the sign of the Cross in a slab of stone or rock. Passing through Westmeath, St. Patrick founded a cloister at Ath Maigne in Asal (? Mayne in barony of Fore); he marked out with his crozier a flag in the flag-stone, and cut the stone as if it were soft clay.[*]

A similar act is recorded of St. Patrick when travelling through Mayo. It is related in the "Tripartite Life," i., p. 137 : " When Patrick went eastward to Lece Finn, where he made a cross in the stone over Cell Mor [Kilmore, barony of Upper Moy]. The Monk's stone is its name to this day."

That a cross should be named after a particular individual is no proof that he was buried beneath it. Thus we read in the "Rennes Dindsenchas" (*Revue Celtique*, tom. xv., §§ 36–37) : "The Cairn of the Children of Leinster is beside the Moor of Tara to the north." (§ 37) : " To the north is the Cross of Fergus, a holy pilgrim: 'tis he who is in [i.e. whose remains are in] Carraic Cluman beside the Cairn of the Children."

That, in very exceptional cases, standing Crosses were sepulchral, is shown by the following story from a homily on the Life of St. Patrick,[†] in which it is clear that the Cross alluded to was an upright monument which he would have naturally seen at a distance, not a mere sign incised on a slab :—

" It was a custom of Patrick's to make the sign of the Cross of Christ over himself a hundred times every day and every night. And whether he were in a chariot or on a horse, he used to fare to every cross, and he would go from his path, even though the cross were distant a thousand paces, provided he saw it or knew that it was near. Now once, on a certain day, Patrick omitted to visit a cross that was on his road, and he knew not that it was there. At the end of the day his charioteer said to him, 'Thou hast left a cross to-day on thy path without visiting it.' (Thereupon) Patrick left the guest-house and his dinner, and went back to the cross. While Patrick was praying at the cross, 'This is a grave,' saith Patrick ; 'Who has been buried here ?' Out of the grave the corpse answered : ' A wretched heathen,' saith he, ' am I. I was buried here. Whilst I was alive I was hurting my soul, and I fell while doing so, and I was then buried here.' ' What was the cause,' saith Patrick, ' of setting on thy grave the symbol of the Christians, namely, the cross ?' ' Not hard to say,' saith he ; ' A certain woman was dwelling in a distant land, and, in her absence, her son was buried here, in this country. And she came from distant lands, and set the cross on this grave. It seemed to her she put it on her son's grave. She was unable, through the grief, to recognise the grave of her son.' Saith Patrick, ' That is why I passed the cross, because it is on the heathen's grave.' Then the cross was set up by Patrick on the grave of the Christian son."

The conclusions to be drawn from these extracts are, generally, that the ancient Sanctuaries were marked by High Crosses outside the ramparts, and that they were under the invocation of certain saints, and offered protection to the fugitive who sought shelter under their arms.

---

[*] *Tripartite Life*, p. 81. [†] *Op. cit.*, p. 135.

That the original founders of our cashels and monasteries carefully planned and thought out every detail with regard to the position these Sanctuary Crosses were to occupy in their monastery, along with their intention and use, is illustrated in the curious drawing

with inscriptions on fol. 95 of the "Book of St. Mulling," of which a facsimile is annexed. It seems impossible not to accept the suggestion put forward by Mr. Olden,* and confirmed in the learned work of Mr. Lawlor,† that this circular device is a ground-plan of an Irish monastery, showing the positions in which the Crosses are to stand; that the Crosses on this plan represent actual stone or wooden Crosses erected on the ground, and that these Crosses were equivalent to an invocation of the prophets and evangelists after whom they are named, viz. :—

| Daniel, | Jeremiah, | Isaiah, | Ezekiel. |
| Matthew, | Mark, | Luke, | John. |

Mr. Olden also suggests that such Crosses may be marked in the ground-plan to indicate the sites of the monastic buildings outside the Vallum, and refers to the passage in the life of St. Fintan, otherwise called Munnu, where the founder is said to have marked seven places in which afterwards the chief buildings of his city should be erected, and he placed Crosses there : "and," Mr. Lawlor adds (p. 173), "this leads to the further inference, that the buildings within the ramparts were dedicated, like modern churches, to the persons of the Blessed Trinity." The discovery of this circular device and its interpretation are of immense value in support of the theory that the Irish High Crosses were not sepulchral, but signs to mark the limits of the Sanctuary.

Mr. Lawlor's transcription of the lines of writing that run round outside the two circles, which may be held to represent the walls or embankments of the rath, is as follows :—

> " 1. (Outer circle of writing). + cros maire ⟦ande⟧e + matt aniar
> + cros ⟦io⟧han ⟦§ husith⟧ + cros lu⟦o − −⟧
> ⟦anoi⟧r
>
> 2. (Inner circle of writing). + ⟦ano⟧irdes+cros heremiæ et aniardes+daniel
> et aniartuaid+eze⟦c⟧A⟦iai −⟧us⟦− −a⟧s⟦o⟧irthu-
> aid + cros ⟦esaiæ⟧

---

* See Dict. of National Biography, vol. xli., p. 48.　　　† See Book of Mulling : Edinburgh, 1897. p. 169.　　　§ ? [antuaith] .

" Taking next the lines within the circles in their order, we have—

    3. +[c]ros í spirta [n]oib

    4. — — — — gm danaib +

    5. + — — caingleib andas

    6. U — — — — t.

    7. +[c]riet conaapatalaib

    8. — — — —å — ~ s

" The following is a translation :—

    1. + Cross of Mark   south   + Matthew   west

       + cross of John   north   + cross of Luke   east

    2. On the south-east + cross of Jeremiah, and on the south-west + Daniel,

       and on the north-west + Ezekiel [— — —], on the north-east + cross of

       [Isaiah].

    3. + Cross of the Holy Spirit.

    4. — — — — — — — — with gifts +

    5. + — — with angels from above.

    6. ?

    7. + Christ with his apostles.

    8. ? "

Mr. Lawlor then discusses the question as to the point at which the inscriptions begin, whether at the south-west or the north-east, and he is inclined to arrive at the conclusion that No. 1 should be read backwards, beginning at Matthew, south-west, when we get the conventional order of the Gospels—Matthew, Mark, Luke, John.

This is beginning at the west, and proceeding left-wise round by south, and east to north. The order in which the Prophets are named will then be Daniel, Jeremiah, Isaiah, and Ezekiel.

This order corresponds with that in the prayer of Colga Ua Duinechda,* which he quotes (p. 170):—

"I beseech with Thee, O Jesus holy, thy four Evangelists who wrote thy Gospel divine, to wit, Matthew, Mark, Luke, John. I beseech with Thee, Thy four chief prophets who foretold Thy incarnation, Daniel, Jeremiah, Isaias, and Ezekiel."

"The whole structure of the prayer," writes Mr. Lawlor, "makes it clear that, by naming in succession the evangelists and the major prophets, the writer intended to suggest a parallel between them," and, he also remarks, "that this fashion of pairing together saints of different eras, 'who were of one manner of life,' was congenial to the Celtic mind, is manifest from the lists preserved in the 'Book of Leinster' and elsewhere," and that "in these lists, prominent Irish saints are compared with saints of the universal Church."

---

* In *Yellow Book of Lecan* (T.C.D., H. 2. 18), col. 886. The prayer is also found in Brussels MS., 5100-4. *Mart. of Gorman*, p. ix.

But may it not be asked whether, in this association of the greater Prophets with the Evangelists, a more profound meaning was intended than merely to establish a comparison between the two? If we extend our inquiries beyond the field of Celtic literature to the wider one of Christian Art abroad, we may come to understand the symbolism and the mysticism with which the minds of all these early Christian church-builders were steeped. For instance, in the south windows of Chartres Cathedral, we seem to have the same idea as that which, five centuries before, was in the mind of him who planted and dedicated the sanctuary crosses of St. Mulling's. At Chartres, the Evangelists are borne on the shoulders of the four Greater Prophets; and in one window, the association is the same as in the coupling of our Crosses in this ground-plan. The Evangelist John is supported on the shoulders of Ezekiel the Prophet. The thing signified is the building up of the New Covenant on the foundation of the Old: the fulfilment of Prophecy in the Advent of that Being whose life is recorded by the Evangelists.*

In some instances, the Irish High Crosses were either dedicatory or commemorative. The Cross in Kells church-ard, inscribed "Patricii et Columbae crux," was evidently erected in commemoration of these two saints who lived at different periods. The High Cross at Clonmacnois and the Cross of Tuam, though dedicated to the memory of two Irish kings, were certainly not over their graves.†

Mr. Lawlor brings forward many instances to show that these terminal Crosses were generally under the invocation of certain saints. To these examples we may add that of the inscribed stone of Killnasaggart, where it is stated that Ternoc, son of Ciaran, bequeathed a place under the protection of St. Peter.‡

St. Mulling seems, from the following passage,§ to have found a high Cross under the invocation of Columba. It is from the tale of the "Boromean Tribute." In this curious passage, the church towers as well as the Cross are mentioned. St. Mulling is pursued by enemies: "in hostile guise the North hemmed in Molling, and his associates, and the Saint said: 'May ye be as rocks upon [? over] brown oaks, may ye be as waves on azure waters, may ye be as belfries surmounting churches, and may all this not be a mere fit of dreaming.' Westward then he came to a place where now St. Mullen's Cross is; there he sat down and made certain quatrains: 'Make we here a bellicose down-sitting, rise we up for fight of victory; whosoever shall be under Columbkill's protection, his body shall not be a prey to wolves.'"

* Le P. Ch. Cahier, S. J.: Caractéristiques des Saints, tom. iv., p. 397.

† See Petrie: Christian Inscriptions, vol. ii., p. 141.

‖ Petrie: op. cit., vol. ii., p. 27.

§ The Tribute: "Silva Gadelica," translated by S. H. O'Grady, vol. ii., p. 428.

There is another point to be observed which, it may be hoped, will help to confirm the suggestions put forth on the meaning of the circular device (*antea*, p. x). Since Mr. Olden first examined the page in St. Mulling's MS. on which it is found, chemicals have been applied to it, and the result has been that some lines, before invisible, have appeared. I think it is quite possible now to trace the outline of the entrance to the Cashel; and it is significant that this entrance is marked as close to the Cross of Christ with his Apostles, reminding us of the words "I am the Door." It is also most interesting that such a Cross has been found at St. Mulling's, and is *in situ*, and on the identical spot marked in the old ground-plan on the east of the enclosure.

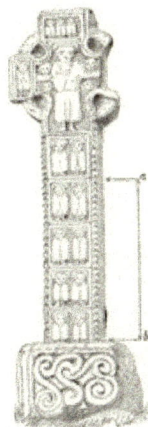

Cross of Christ with the Apostles, St. Mulling's.

In the accompanying drawing, I have attempted a restoration of this Cross, marking, by a line, the restored portion. Allowing for one figure in the right and left arm panels, it will be seen that the grouping of the figures of the other ten Apostles in the panels exactly corresponds with that on the south side of the South Cross of Castledermot, where we have the Apostles in six groups of two each.

Christ and the Apostles are represented either in groups of three or four on the Crosses of Kilcullen, Moone, and Clonmacnois. May it not be supposed that they occupied the same position and were under the same dedication as that at the east of St. Mulling's, in the annexed ground-plan? Unfortunately, few of these Crosses are in situ; this shows how important it is to inquire into every fact as to their original position in the church-yard. It is impossible to look at the spirals on the base of this Cross at St. Mulling's without being reminded of those on the base of the North Cross of Castledermot. Both belong to an archaic style which writers such as Mr. Coffey, who have made prehistoric Art in Ireland their special study, will agree with me in thinking is much more like the spirals at the entrance of New Grange than the double spirals we see on the eleventh and twelfth century Crosses of Ireland. This resemblance may point to the period when pagan Art was passing into Christian. The date of the manuscript in which this ground-plan of St. Mulling's occurs is held by scholars

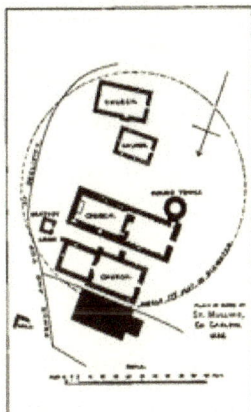

to belong to the ninth century (A.D. 800–900), the original having been written in the seventh century (A.D. 600–700).

The date of the foundation of Castledermot is *circa* 650, and that in which its school flourished under Snedgus is *circa* 850. May it not be suggested that the archaic Cross which corresponds to that of St. Mulling's, in the character of its art, may belong to the period of the foundation of the church, and the South Cross—so much more advanced in style—to the period of Snedgus and Cormac, i.e. *circa* 850 to 900.

One point appears to me to have been missed by Mr. Olden and Mr. Lawlor in their examination of this circular device or ground-plan, and that is, that although only two circles are visible, yet the external inscriptions run in two distinct circles, and the lines on which they run may have been in a different and more fugitive colour.

Again, the three Crosses (there is a fourth Cross, not named, and which stands in the hollow between the two ridges of the circular enclosure) were apparently dedicated to the three Persons of the Trinity, within the Sanctuary, and are so placed that, if a circle was drawn so as to pass through the centre of each Cross, we should have three circles to add to the other four, and so arrive at the mystic number—seven: the outer circle being allotted to Christ with His Apostles, the next to the Holy Ghost, with the seven gifts of the Spirit; the third to the Father, with angels from above. It is impossible to consider this without being reminded of the Symbolism of the Mystic Circles in which theologians, poets, and architects, of early Christian times indicated the luminous spheres that lead us up to God: such as the Byzantine dome with its circle above circle; the wheel windows of French cathedrals, where, painted on the glass and sculptured on the mullions, Heaven is reflected on the face of the Sanctuary; or the snow-white rose in the vision of Dante, wherein were ranged the Sacred Host in circle above circle until we reach the Empyrean.

In the Laurentian Library of Florence there is a manuscript poem by Matteo Palmieri, illuminated (as many have thought) by Botticelli. The poem is named, "Citta di Vita," and the illustration is a diagram much the same in character as this "circular device." Is it a fair suggestion to make, that even while believing the circular device, found in St. Mulling's book, to have been a ground plan of his monastery, it was also a diagram of that City of Life which formed the ideal of his Sanctuary?

THE CASTLEDERMOT CROSSES.

THE DURROW CROSS.

CASTLEDERMOT MONASTERY is situated in the county of Kildare, barony of Kilkea and Moone. The name of this place was originally Disert Diarmada, or the hermitage of Dermod. The word Disert has been corrupted into Tristle, and so the place was named Tristledermot in the middle ages.

The founder of the church here is said to have been Diarmait, who is commemorated in the Irish martyrologies on the 21st of June. He is also named Ainle, i.e. "delightful his colour," in the martyrology of Oengus. His genealogy is given in the "Book of Lecan," at folio 72.

The earliest date at which Castledermot is mentioned in the "Annals of the Four Masters," is A.D. 841—the plundering of Disert Diarmada by the foreigners of Cael-uisc (Archdall). From the middle of the ninth century to the year of his death, in 885, the abbot Sneidghius, wise man of Disert Diarmada, tutor of Cormac, son of Cuilennan, flourished here. This Cormac was a prince, afterwards Bishop of Cashel. He is said to have been author of the "Sanas Cormaic," and to have assisted in settling a moot point in the Brehon Law. The Irish annals record the deaths of four more abbots of Castledermot respectively, under the dates 874, 884, 919, 921, 935, 943, 963, 967, and 1074. An Colgan relates that the Abbey was again pillaged in the year 1040.[*] In the reign of King John, a priory was founded outside the walls, and, in 1302, a Franciscan Friary was founded here by the Lord of Offaly.[†]

The ruins of Castledermot Monastery, still remaining, are the chancel-arch and a portion of the wall of the Irish romanesque church, the Cloictech, or Bell-house, which belongs to the oldest style of these buildings, being characterised by rough masonry and square-headed apertures. The holy well is dedicated to St. James, who is now the patron of the parish of Castledermot. A perforated stone, and bronze bell, now preserved at Kilkea Castle, were found here.

Church and Round Tower at Castledermot. Drawn by George Petrie LL.D. From T. Cromwell's "Excursions in Ireland," vol. iii.

The two high Crosses, with the round tower, appear to be the oldest monument of this sanctuary. The Crosses stand one to the north, and the other to the south of the

---

* Tr. Thaum. cap. xx., p. 658.   † See *Journal of the Co. Kildare Archæological Society*, vol. i., pp. 361-378.

old church. The north Cross, which is evidently the older of the two, is *in situ*. It stands west of the round tower, and north of the church. Both these Crosses are formed of granite, which is the stone of the district.

THE NORTH CROSS.

The north Cross, base included, is ten feet three inches high. It measures three feet ten inches across the arms. The shaft measures sixteen inches across the face, and eleven inches in thickness. The plinth, which measures three feet in height, by two feet eight inches in width at the base, has two panels on each face, while the west face of the Cross itself is divided into seven panels, and those on the face of the circle being added, make thirteen panels in all. The whole Cross is cut out of one stone.* The roofing-stone, which would have probably added eighteen inches to the height, has been lost.

The subjects in these panels are as follows :—

WEST FACE.

1, 2. Base—Double Spiral.	7. Martyrdom of St. Peter.
3. Three Figures.	8. Sacrifice of Isaac.
4. Three Figures.	9. David with his Harp.
5. Daniel in Lions' Den.	10—13. Scrolls and Interlacings.†
6. Fall of Man.	

EAST FACE.

1, 2. Double Spirals.	5. Crucifixion.
3. Two Figures.	6—9. Twelve Apostles in four groups
4. Abraham and Melchisedek.	of three.

SOUTH SIDE.

1. Miracle of Loaves and Fishes.   2. Spiral Design.   3. Interlaced Scroll.

NORTH SIDE.

1. Figure of Death.	3. Double Spiral.
2. Interlacing.	4. Figure at Prayer.

The figure on the base at the north side, which we believe to symbolise death, appears to represent a pagan, and not a Christian, interment. The emaciated form is seated and swathed, his arms clasping his knees. In the "Painter's Guide of Mount Athos," it is

---

* The clasping-out of the Castledermot Crosses has not always been executed by the carvers with perfect accuracy. It is this that makes the perspective of some of the openings to appear slightly incorrect, or inconsistent, in the illustrations. In the views of both *faces* of the north Castledermot Cross, the arm to the observer's left looks much thicker than the other one; this is particularly striking in the view of the east face of the Cross. The reason is, that the soffit, or under side, of the south arm of this Cross, instead of being horizontal, slopes laterally downwards towards the west, as is shown in the illustration of the north *side*, or edge, of the Cross. This makes that arm look

thicker than the other, as seen from the east, and thinner than the other, as seen from the west, the height of the photographic camera being less than that of the under surface of the arm.—ED.

† The ornamentation of the quadrants, as we may take leave to call them, on the west face of the north Cross at Castledermot is now so indistinct, that it seemed prudent not to attempt to restore it in the illustration. There may be room for difference of opinion as to the decipherment of the designs on the two right-hand quadrants on the east face of the Cross, but none at all respecting the two left-hand ones, whose patterns are unmistakable.—ED.

ordered that, when the Crucifixion of Christ is represented (as we see it on the west face of this cross), a hollow or cave tomb should be shown at the base of the cross, in which the bones of Adam appear washed by the blood that falls from the feet of Christ.

The accompanying figure represents the sitting posture in an interment described by Mr. Thomas Bateman, in his "Ten years' Diggings in Celtic and Saxon Grave-hills in the Counties of Derby, Stafford, and York," p. 22. This skeleton was found in opening a cairn near Parcelly Hay Wharf of the Cromford and High Peak Railway. "The body had been placed upright in a sitting or crouching posture, as was abundantly evident from the order in which the bones were found."

It seems probable that the attitude was, originally, the same as that represented in the north side of the Cross (see Plate), and that the arms were clasped round the legs and held in position by such bandages or cords as we see represented in the sculptured figure on the Cross. Remains of such cords, used for supporting the dead in position, were found by M. Tschudi of Glaris (during his scientific expedition to Peru) upon some mummies, where the legs were drawn up to the chest, and the arms folded.

In the figure represented on Castledermot north Cross, the cords or bandages used for the purposes of keeping the skeleton in its position are carefully represented; and the whole subject is most valuable and interesting as illustrating the position and method of binding the corpse while the skeleton was still clothed with flesh. The questions suggested by this image are :—

Did the sculptor of this figure draw from his imagination or from memory ? Was this form of interment practised in Ireland to a comparatively late period ?*

This figure may be taken as the prelude to the drama which opens at the Fall of man.† On panel 6 of the west face of the Cross, Adam and Eve are represented eating the forbidden fruit, the serpent twining up the stem of a tree. In Byzantine art the tree is the fig-tree ; in northern art it is an apple-tree, as it appears to be here.

On panel 8 of the west face, the redemption is prefigured by the sacrifice of Isaac— as we read in the words of the " Biblia Pauperum," " The father sacrifices his son, who typifies Christ."

On panel 9, David with his harp foretells the redemption of man.

---

* See *Man, the primeval Savage*, p. 680, by Worthington G. Smith : 1894.

† In Domenico Beccafumi's painting of the " Descent into Hell," A.D. 1484–1549, a Promethean form, on the cavern floor, is to be seen rising as Christ appears above with cross and banner. It represents Adam awakening from Death at the sight of the Saviour ; and the same figure, issuing from the tomb, is one of the subjects on a thirteenth-century window in Beauvais cathedral, in the chapel of the Blessed Virgin. A grave filled with bones, soon to be resuscitated, is often shown in ancient art—below the crucifixion. This is prescribed in the Byzantine manual.—*Christian Iconography*, vol. ii., p. 106, Didron : ed. M. Stokes. See D'Agincourt, *Peinture*, vol. v., pl. LIX., 1. fig. 6.

On panel 5, Daniel in the den of lions is the favourite symbol (along with the three children in the furnace), seen in the "Art of the Catacombs" to signify triumph over suffering. In the "Mount Athos Guide," it is directed that he should stand in the midst of seven lions, as stated in the apocryphal book, Bel and the Dragon, verse 32. In the "Biblia Pauperum," this subject is a type of Christ's resurrection and triumph over death.

On panel 7, west face, the figure head-downmost, between two soldiers, may signify the martyrdom of St. Peter, as prescribed by the "Mount Athos Guide"—"St. Peter crucified upside down—his head down, his feet upwards—soldiers encircle him; some nail his hands, others his feet." *

On panel 1, on south side of the plinth, the miracle of loaves and fishes—a subject prescribed in the "Mount Athos Guide," and appearing in the "Art of the Catacombs," as a type of the Lord's Supper—on the south side of the Cross.

On the east face, panel 4, Melchisedek comes before Abraham, arrayed in sacerdotal vestment, holding plate and chalice of wine as prescribed by the "Mount Athos Guide," a subject used in the "Speculum," and also in the "Biblia Pauperum," as a type of the Lord's Supper. The "Mount Athos Guide" directs that it should be treated thus—"The righteous Melchisedek, arrayed in a sacerdotal vestment, holds plate and chalice of wine. Abraham, dressed as a warrior, stands before him." And the "Biblia Pauperum" adds— "In the 14th chapter of Genesis, when Abraham returned from the slaughter of his enemies, bringing with him much spoil, which he had wrested from his enemies, then Melchisedek, the high priest of God, brought him bread and wine. Melchisedek is a type of Christ who at supper gave to His disciples bread and wine—that is, His body and blood—to eat and drink." And in the "Speculum Humanæ Salvationis," this subject is ordered as prophetic of the Last Supper, along with those of the rain of Manna and the Jews eating the Paschal Lamb. Here the prophetic subjects on this Cross close, and are followed by the great scene of the final act of Redemption, the death of Christ on the Cross, and His Church bearing witness in the groups of the Twelve Apostles standing round the Cross. A soldier Longinus pierces the right side of Christ; another soldier holds a sponge attached to the end of the rod, which he holds to the mouth of Christ, as directed by the "Mount Athos Guide" and the "Biblia Pauperum."

The question as to the date of this Cross can only be decided by comparison with those monuments, the age of which has been already approximately fixed: and we may presume that this north Cross at Castledermot belongs to an earlier period than those of Clonmacnois and Monasterboice, which are held to belong to the beginning of the tenth century. The character of the art displayed on the north Cross at Castledermot, along with the whole aspect of the monument, indicates greater antiquity than that of the south Cross in the same churchyard.

No ancient references to this monument have been found, nor have I been able to discover any existing legend or superstition connected with it.

---

* This may represent the death of Isaiah, a type in the *Speculum Humanæ Salvationis*, for the crucifixion of Christ.   Isaiah hung and sawn in two, illustrates a Rabbinical tradition that he was thus punished because he said he had seen God.

As to its present condition, this monument is more weather-worn, and its sculptures have been more smoothed away by time, than those on any High Cross I have yet seen.

I do not know of any previous illustrations of this Cross having appeared. The panel on the south side of the Cross is illustrated, in outline, by Mr. Romilly Allen, at page 225 of his work " On early Christian symbolism in Great Britain and Ireland," and the panel on the north side of the base is given at page 282 of the " Journal of the Archæological Society of the County Kildare," vol. i.

THE SOUTH CROSS.

The South Cross, base included, stands fourteen feet three inches high. It measures three feet four inches across the arms. The shaft measures fifteen inches across the face, and is nine inches in thickness. The plinth, which measures two feet nine inches in height, by three feet in width, has one panel on the western and another on the southern side, while the north side is divided into three panels, only one of which was sculptured. This side of the base is evidently unfinished, and on the east face the sculptor had not even commenced his work.

This Cross is in three pieces—the arms, head, and circle being cut from one block, while the shaft and plinth form two separate blocks.

The subjects in these panels are as follows :—

WEST FACE.

1. Noah entering the Ark.
2. Daniel in the Den of Lions.
3. Three Figures, two with animal heads.
4. The Fall of Man.
5. Abraham and Melchisedek.
6. Crucifixion.
7. Sacrifice of Isaac.
8. David with his Harp.
9, 10. Three Figures.
11—14. Scrolls on face of circle.

EAST FACE.

1. Plinth—no design.
2. Divergent Spirals.
3. Diagonal Fret.
4. Double Spiral.
5. Interlaced Knot.
6. Diagonal Patterns.
7. Divergent Spiral.

NORTH SIDE.

1. Figure at Prayer.
2. Two Figures (? Prophet and Evangelist).
3. (?) St. Matthew and his Angel.
4. (?) Evangelist with Sword and Shield.
5. Jacob wrestling with Angel.
6. (?) Figure of Ecclesiastic.
7. Double Spiral.
8. On Plinth—Unfinished Group.

SOUTH SIDE.

1. Two Apostles.
2. Two Apostles.
3. Two Apostles.
4. Two Apostles.
5. Two Apostles.
6. Two Apostles.
7. On plinth—Miracle of Loaves and Fishes.
8. Double Spiral.
9. Figure of Ecclesiastic.

It will be seen that, on this Cross, there are eight of the same subjects as on the north Cross, though treated in a very different manner, while we have four new subjects on the north side of the shaft. Thus we have on the base, Noah entering the Ark. In the art of the Catacombs, the deluge, signified by Noah entering the Ark, prefigured baptism, but this type does not occur in the "Biblia Pauperum" or the "Speculum." In the "Mount Athos Guide," we read—"Fallow beasts and birds and all kinds of animals enter the Ark." Noah is the third patriarchal type of our Lord, the Ark is a type of the Church, and the whole story is used by St. Peter (1 Ep. iii. 20-21), Tertullian, and other Fathers of the Church, as prefiguring baptism.

On panel 2, on the west face, we have Daniel in the Den of Lions : here only four lions are given. They are placed perpendicularly at each side of the figure of the Prophet, who stands erect and is clothed. The whole treatment of this subject, though not exactly similar, reminds us strongly of the damascened Christian ornaments illustrated by Le Blant, in his work on Christian Inscriptions.* In both, Daniel is standing in prayer between lions who lick his arms, and head, or feet ; and although Le Blant states that the prophet is almost universally represented as naked, yet in every instance on these Irish monuments he is clothed. Indeed Le Blant seems to contradict himself, since he gives ten instances of representations of Daniel with the lions in early Christian art where the prophet's figure is clothed. Emeric David says that, before the Sixteenth Council, held A.D. 1414, this figure was always represented in Art as clothed.

This upright form of Daniel in prayer prefigures Resurrection, signifying that as God has delivered him from lions, so has He delivered us from death.

Panel 7.—The Sacrifice of Isaac is called "Sacrifice of Abraham" in the "Byzantine Painter's Guide," where the following directions are given : Abraham is to hold the Sacrificial knife, while his son Isaac is shown tied upon the wood ; an angel points to the lamb caught by the horns in a bush. At the foot, two youths hold an ass harnessed. In the "Biblia Pauperum," Isaac kneels unbound on an altar—this and the serpent lifted in the wilderness being the types of Crucifixion. In the "Speculum," the father holds the son by the head ; Isaac bears his load of faggots as in the fine fresco of the same subject in the cemetery of Priscilla, in the Catacombs. In the Irish treatment of the subject, Isaac lays his head upon the block, and does not appear to have been bound to it.

Panel 6.—The Crucifixion, with lance and sponge. Longinus, the Roman centurion, pierces the right side of Christ ; the soldier Stephaton holds the sponge to his mouth ; both soldiers stand beside the Cross. The feet of Christ are separate, so that four nails, not three, would be the number of these instruments of the Passion. The treatment of the subject varies in this instance from the directions in the "Byzantine Guide," where it is directed that the soldiers are to be represented on horseback ; while in the "Biblia Pauperum" and "Speculum," their presence is not indicated in the text. Nevertheless, this treatment of the subject on the Irish Cross appears to have been a very usual and

---

* Inscriptions Chrétiennes de la Gaule antérieure au VIII* siècle : Edmond Le Blant, Paris : vol. i, plate 43, figs. 248-252 and vol. ii, plate 87, fig. 519.

ancient method of representing the Crucifixion, and is found in early miniatures, enamels, and ivories of the ninth century.

Panel 8.—David and his Harp. Said to be one of the closest types of Christ and of his power over the human soul afforded in Scripture, as he calms the fury of Saul by his music. This image occurs all through early Christian and mediæval art. The harp here represented, like D reversed, is a very primitive form of the instrument.

The subject of the second panel on the north side, presuming it to be intended for prophet and evangelist, may illustrate the practice of Irish saints having a *fer imchuir*, or bearer. The most primæval mode of carriage by land, namely on a human being's back, is exemplified in the Life of St. Patrick,[*] where the saint's foster-father carries him home; in the Life of St. Brigit, where a man carries his consumptive mother to her to be healed; in the Life of St. Findian, where Murodach carries St. Findian over three fields; and, in that of St. Ciaran, where his bearer (*fer imchuir*) is mentioned; St. Patrick employed his champion, Mac Cairtheun, for a similar purpose.[†]

Another explanation of the subject in this panel is suggested by a comparison with the pictures, already alluded to (see Introduction, p. xii.), on the great window of the Cathedral of Chartres. Here the four Evangelists are shown as seated on the shoulders of the four greater Prophets, and the figures in the other panels, on this side of the Cross, may be figures of Evangelists—one, especially, with a shield and sword, may well stand for St. Matthew.

With regard to the unfinished panel on the north side of the base of this Cross, it is evident that the sculptor was interrupted in his work.

No ancient reference to this monument has as yet been found, nor have I been able to discover any existing legend or superstition connected with it. In its present condition, it is much less injured than most of the High Crosses that I have yet seen in Ireland.

An illustration, in outline, of the west face of this Cross forms the frontispiece of the work of Mr. J. Romilly Allen, on "Early Christian Symbolism in Great Britain and Ireland." At page 225 of the same work, the miracle of the loaves and fishes, as sculptured on the south side of the base of this Cross, is illustrated.

---

* W. Stokes: *Lives of the Saints from the Book of Lismore*, pp. c, 152, 191, 224, 275.　　† *Tripartite Life*, p. 174.

The Window of the Lady Chapel, in the Franciscan Abbey, Castledermot.
George Petrie, LL.D. From T. Cromwell's "Excursions in Ireland," ed. ii.

THE DURROW CROSS.

Durrow is situated in the townland and parish of that name, in the north of the King's County, and on the borders of Westmeath.

The name is derived from the Irish Dermag, signifying Oak-plain. Ross grencha was another ancient name of this place. It originally formed part of the territory of Fir-cell, which was included in the kingdom of Teffia.

The church was founded here by Saint Columcille in the sixth century. We read in the ecclesiastical history of the venerable Bede : " Fecerat autem priusquam Brittaniam veniret, monasterium nobile in Hibernia, quod a copia roborum Dearmach lingua Scottorum, hoc est, campus roborum cognominatur."—See Dr. Reeves' " Adamnan," p. 23, note b. " Before he passed over into Britain, he built a noble monastery in Ireland, which, from the great number of oaks, is, in the Scottish tongue, called Dearmach, the field of oaks."[*]

When Columba was at Durrow, he is said to have done three things. He built a chapel or cell there, he sweetened the apples that grew in the country round (by miracle), and he sent a charmed sword to Colman Mor, son of Diarmait,[*] whose death is recorded in the " Annals of the Four Masters," A.D. 552.

The Crosses of Durrow are referred to in the following verses of a poem attributed to St. Columba, found among the McClery manuscripts in Brussels[†] :—

> " O Cormac, beautiful is thy church,
> With its books, and learning ;
> A devout city with a hundred crosses,
> Without blemish, without transgression ;
> A holy dwelling confirmed by my verse,
> The green of Aedh, son of Brenann,
> The oak-plain of far-famed Ross-grencha :
> The night upon which her pilgrimage collect,
> In numbers unknown to any but only God."

The hundred Crosses mentioned as within this holy city, probably include the sepulchral slabs marked with Crosses along with the High Crosses on the boundary of the Sanctuary.

The existing remains of the Monastery are very few and difficult to trace. The middle of the cemetery is occupied by a disused Protestant church, in the wall of the east gable

---

[*] See *Lives of the Saints from the Book of Lismore*, p. 174. [†] See Dr. Reeves' *Adamnan*, p. 764, note a, and p. 289.

of which a fragment of a mediæval crucifixion is inserted. The base of an old Cross, with an empty socket, lies outside the graveyard to the south-east. Three tombstones with decorated Crosses of the Early Irish style, one of which is inscribed Ōr do Aigidiu, and another Ōr do Chathalan, are to be found within the cemetery.*

It would appear that there was once an Irish Romanesque church here, from various fragments lying about in the grass, such as a block of stone, probably a portion of a pilaster, covered with interlaced ornaments, and the top of a round-headed window, with bold mouldings, which is now inserted in the wall of the churchyard.

The High Cross of Durrow stands to the west of the now disused church. It is made of sandstone. It is not *in situ.* The whole monument, from the base to the top of the roofing stone, is twelve feet in height. It measures four feet and a quarter in width across the arms. The plinth, which is half buried in the ground, measures two feet in height, it is four feet wide at the base, and two feet wide at the top. It is perfectly plain all round. There are twelve panels on the west face, the subjects in which are as follows :—

West Face.

1. Crucifixion, with Lance and Sponge.	5, 6, 7, 8. Spiral and Interlaced Designs.
2. Two Figures and a Bird—One holding Cornucopia.	9. Three Figures.
	10. Figure seized by Two Armed Men.
3. Figure holding (?) a Mirror.	11. (?) Seizure of Christ in Gethsemane.
4. Dove.	12. Soldiers at the Tomb of Christ.

East Face.

1. Triumph of Christ.	6. Agnus Dei.
2. (?) David playing on Lyre.	7. Sacrifice of Isaac.
3. David and the Lion.	8. Interlacings.
4. The Lamb Redeemed.	9. (?) The Trinity, with Angels above.
5. Figure with Hands raised in Prayer.	10, 11, 12. Panels at terminations of Arms, Interlaced Work.

North Side.

1. Double Spiral and Triquetra.	5. Double Spiral.
2. Seated Figure.	6. Jacob wrestling.
3. Billet Moulding encircling Heads.	7. Panel with Inscription.
4. Two Figures.	

South Side.

1. Pattern destroyed.	5. Cain and Abel.
2. Man on Horseback.	6. The Fall of Man.
3. Billet Moulding.	7. (?) Two Griffins.
4. Crowned Figure with Two Dogs.	

* See Petrie: *Christian Inscriptions*, vol. ii., p. 54, plate xxxi.

B

In panel 1, west face, the treatment of the Crucifixion is the same as in most of the Irish High Crosses, the figures bearing lance and sponge being at either side of the Saviour. In panel 4, the Holy Spirit hovers over the Saviour's head in the form of a dove. The circular object held by the figure, in panel 3, may be meant for a mirror—a common funereal symbol in antiquity. The subjects in the other panels, on this side, are all connected with the Passion of Our Lord.

The subjects on the east face appear, generally, to symbolise the Resurrection. In panel 1 the Saviour is seen standing and clothed, holding a sceptre in His right hand, probably the blossoming rod of Aaron, and in His left, the Cross. The joys of Heaven are symbolised in the forms by which His figure is surrounded—musicians with trumpet and lyre; the redemption of the Lamb and the type of redemption—the sacrifice of Isaac.

In panel 4, on the south side, special notice should be taken of the figure seated on the throne, wearing a lunula as crown, holding a sword in his right hand, and a spear in his left, and having an Irish wolf-dog at each side of his throne. May it not be possible that here we have a representation of the King Colman the Great, son of Dermod, to whom Saint Columba sent his sained sword, and "the virtue that lay in that sword was, that no one could die in its presence." In any case, the figure is of great value, as an illustration of ancient costume.

On the east face of the Cross, the instrument held by the musician, to the right of the Saviour's figure, is noteworthy. It has been hitherto mistaken for a harp, but after long examination and much labour and pains taken to procure an accurate rubbing, it became clear that this instrument was a lyre, rather than a harp—but a lyre so peculiar in form that it was not until I had consulted such authorities as Mr. Hipkins, Mr. Culwick, and Mr. Quarry, that I ventured to present this illustration of it, or to name it as such. Mr. Hipkins observes : "It is obviously a cithara, the essential part of which instrument

Musicians on Cross of Durrow.

is the sound-body, or resonance-box. The bridge is Greek in principle, and it is placed so as to carry the vibrations of the strings to the sound-body. This bridge is set rather obliquely, so that, as in the classical cithara, the shortest and highest note comes nearest the player, the deepest note being that farthest away from him. There were only six strings on this instrument, as is frequently the case in the lyres represented on the Greek vases, although seven was the usual number. The left arm of the player is partly concealed by the cithara sound-body."

This instrument is new to Mr. Hipkins, who, as his writings testify, is a learned authority on the history of ancient musical instruments, but he thinks it looks like a transition instrument from which the Irish harp might have been evolved by increasing the number of strings and attaching them in the modern harp fashion to a sound-body removed to the back. It is possible that the origin of such an instrument may be traceable to the primitive kissar, found in Egypt and Abyssinia, the next to which would be the Greek lyre in its perfected form, cithara, of which the Welsh crwt may be a variety. However, in its later form, this instrument was played with the bow, not with the finger or plectrum, as was the method with the lyre, and with this Durrow instrument. The crwt required two drone strings, akin to the Italian lyra, and later on, the theorbo.

Finally, this Durrow lyre-harp may represent a transition instrument from a cithara to a harp, when the harp might have been evolved by increasing the number of strings, and attaching them in modern harp-fashion to a sound-body removed to the back. Mr. Culwick adds: "This is certainly not a harp, but it resembles a rotta, which is an instrument of the middle ages, with an affinity to the kissar, and also to the kinnor."[*]

Traces of an inscription may be found in the lowest panels of the shaft on the north side and west face. The only letters now to be deciphered are:—

OR DO M...ARO......RT (? G) ⊔⊔⊔⊔ .

(OR D)O DUBT(ACH)⊔⊔—⊔⊔—⊔⊔⊔⊔ .

In the "Annals of the Four Masters," we read of a steward of Durrow, named Dubtach, son of Iarnain:—

"A.D. 1010. Dubhthach, son of Iarnan, Airchinnech of Dermag, died."

The same event is recorded in the "Chronicles of Hy":—

"A.D. 1010. Dubhthaich mac Iarnain, Airchinnech de Dairmagh, died."

If we assume that the letters on the west face of the Cross are a portion of the name of this steward of Durrow, we may rank this Cross, erected to his memory in

---

* Since this went to Press, I have found an illustration of a similar instrument sculptured on a capital in the Abbatial Church of Cluny.—See Annales Archéologiques: ed. Didron, Paris, tom. xvi., p. 90.

A.D. 1010, with the following monuments whose dates seem to have been approximately fixed :—

The sculptured slabs at Clonmacnois of Odran Ua h-Eolais, died 994[*]; of Flanchad, Bishop of Clonmacnois, d. 1002[†]; of Corpre MacCathail of Glendalough, d. A.D. 1013[‡]; the churches built by King Brian Boruma, at Killaloe[§] and Iniscaltra[‖]; the Bell-house of Kinneth, built by Abbot Mocholmog, A.D. 1015[¶]; the Gospels of Dubinse of Bangor, in the library of Corpus Christi, Oxford[**]; the shrine of St. Molash's book, wrought by Gillabaithin, in 1001[††]; and the Shrine of the Stowe Missal, wrought by Dunchad O'Taccain in 1023.[‡‡]

A woodcut of the east face of Durrow Cross was published by Mr. Marcus Keane in his work on the "Towers and Tombs of Ancient Ireland." Drawings by George Petrie, LL.D., of two inscribed Stones at Durrow, were published in 1872, in "Christian Inscriptions in the Irish Language," vol. ii., p. 56, plate 31 : there is also the above-mentioned drawing of the east face of the Cross on page 55. Outlines from measured drawings and rubbings of Durrow High Cross have been published by Mr. Thomas J. Westropp, in illustration of a paper "On the Old Graveyards in Durrow Parish," by the Rev. S. de Courcy Williams, M.A., in the "Journal of the Royal Society of Antiquaries of Ireland," vol. vii., 5th series, pp. 143–7 (1897).

South side of Durrow Cross

North side of Durrow Cross

---

* See Petrie : *Christian Inscriptions*, vol. i., p. 61, plate LIII., fig. 181.

† *Ib.*, fig. 182.

‡ *Op. cit.*, vol. ii., p. 49, plate XXXII.

§ *Notes on Irish Architecture*, by Edwin, Earl of Dunraven, vol. ii., plates CIII. and CIV., p. 87.

‖ *Op. cit.*, plates XCVII. and XCVIII., p. 88.

¶ See Smith : *History of Cork*, vol. ii., p. 407.

** See *National MSS. of Ireland*, Part ii., xxiii. Introd., plates XLVI., XLVII.

†† See Petrie : *Christian Inscriptions*, vol. ii., p. 90, plate XLII., fig. 89.

‡‡ *Op. cit.*, p. 94, fig. 91.

(WEST FACE)　CASTLEDERMOT.—THE SOUTH CROSS.　(EAST FACE)

(WEST FACE)　CASTLEDERMOT.—THE NORTH CROSS.　(EAST FACE)

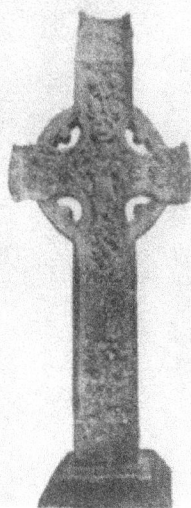

(WEST FACE)　THE DURROW CROSS.　(EAST FACE)

THE CASTLEDERMOT SOUTH CROSS.
(WEST FACE.)

THE CASTLEDERMOT SOUTH CROSS.
EAST FACE.

THE CASTLEDERMOT SOUTH CROSS.
(SOUTH SIDE.)

THE CASTLEDERMOT SOUTH CROSS.

THE DURROW CROSS.
(WEST FACE.)

THE DURROW CROSS.
(EAST FACE.)

THE DURROW CROSS.
(SOUTH SIDE.)

THE DURROW CROSS.
(NORTH SIDE.)